# A MANUAL OF SELF-HEALING

An explanation of how to channel mental energy
using visualization programmes, breathing
techniques and relaxation to instruct the body's
healing processes to overcome a wide range of
common ailments.

# A MANUAL OF SELF-HEALING

*by*

E. H. Shattock

DESTINY BOOKS

ROCHESTER, VERMONT

Destiny Books
1 Park Street
Rochester, Vermont 05767

U.K. edition published by Turnstone Press, Ltd.
Denington Estate, Wellingborough
Northhamptonshire, NN8 2RQ England

LIBRARY OF CONGRESS CATALOGING IN PUBLICATION DATA

Shattock, E.H.
   A manual of self-healing.
   Includes index.
   1. Self-care, Health.   2. Mind and body.
   3. Autogenic training.   4. Mental health.   I. Title.
   RA776.95.S5      615.8      82-2318
   ISBN 0-89281-040-8      AACR2


Manufactured in U.S.A. by W.S. Konecky Assoc.

Destiny Books is a division of Inner Traditions International, Ltd.

10  9  8  7  6  5  4  3

# CONTENTS

# INTRODUCTION

It is six years since I started to work out a technique of self-healing, and five years since the book on the subject, *Mind Your Body*, was written. During those years, I have had daily experience of carrying out a great variety of programmes and gained a lot of information on how to make the treatment more effective. From the many letters I have received as a result of the publicaction of the book and the course I have given on the subject of self-healing by this method, I learnt that a simpler form of presentation is required than that given in the previous book. That is what I have done in this book, and hope that the course of lessons (the early ones dealing with one single aspect of the technique with full explanations, and the later ones with detailed programmes and future possibilities) will enable those, who before were hesitant because of the difficulties and complications I encountered, to study these simple lessons and start out on the exciting venture of healing themselves.

One has to use one's judgement to decide when self-healing is indicated and when the expert attention of one or other of the practitioners in the various branches of medicine should be preferred. There are also many methods of healing, now spoken of as 'fringe medicine', that are readily available. Many of these will, before long, be accepted as legitimate practice. One might find that a severe infection in part of the body was proving resistant to the scavenging action of the phagocytic cells; it is then reasonable to ask the advice of a doctor who may decide to prescribe antibiotics in order to clear it up.

This use of the mind is not a substitute for allopathic medicine, neither is it to be preferred when homoeopathic, osteopathic, chiropractic, acupuncture, electro-, colour or sound therapies are available to help in serious disorders. Sometimes a person would prefer to see a psychic or spiritual healer, and there are those who heal with energy direction and with magnetism. Each of these finds its proper place with particular individuals, but none is to be regarded as a universal remedy.

The self-healing technique which I have developed is just another alternative, but it does have the distinct advantage that it can be carried out, in many cases, entirely on one's own initiative, without troubling a practitioner at all. On many other occasions it will only be necessary to obtain a diagnosis of the trouble. This therapy should, if taken up fairly widely, relieve the medical fraternity of a load of effort now being spent on minor ills which the body, given the necessary encouragement, is perfectly capable of dealing with itself. It can, of course, assist with all the other forms of healing, for instance, after the setting of a broken limb, the repair of torn flesh after an accident, or in overcoming an infection. It is *not* a panacea, but it can adequately deal with all the little ills that so often require a doctor's attention, and quite a number of more serious ones. To what extent this healing method can be successful beyond what I have already found possible, I do not know; we shall only learn this as more people seriously try out the technique, discover additional possibilities and establish its limitations. I expect that some of the limitations I have had to accept at present will be overcome.

The principle employed is the same as that developed by Monsieur Coué, the once popular 'Couéism', but with a more precise expression. There is no doubt that the practice of this technique is, in itself, a fruitful training of the mind in three of the important features that are required to bring its full power into action. These are focus or concentration, mind-picturing and breathing. The result of this training on some people who are ready for further expansion of the mind's powers will be nothing less than sensational, and I use that term deliberately and without exaggeration. The untapped resources of the mind are just waiting to be released, but care has to be taken in the way in which this is done. There are, both in the U.K. and in the U.S.A., courses offerred which, over a week-end, can so develop the psychic perceptions as to propel an individual into a new field of awareness for which he has not been properly prepared. This sudden opening of new mental vision is not always a good thing; in fact, it seldom is. The psychic powers, if they are not to be misused, need to be balanced by a wide and embracing love which extends to all humanity, and they should be acquired naturally and only when the individual has raised his awareness beyond the horizon of his sensual experience.

The technique explained in this course of self-healing is not designed to release psychic powers, but only to build a channel along which enhanced mind power can flow. The energy is thus directed to where it can be of most benefit in keeping the physical vehicle fit for its task in the world and, in certain limited cases, in assisting others to overcome physical defects.

In my previous book, *Mind Your Body*, which recorded the development of this method of using the mind, too much prominence was given to the two main problems I was facing at that time; a seriously enlarged prostate and an advanced arthritic hip. Both these are difficult defects to put right, at any rate, with my present knowledge of how they can be dealt with, and this is reflected by the length of time and by the ups and downs that occurred during the period of treatment. At the time, I did not know what other ills I might be able to treat, or indeed, whether what I was doing for the prostate and hips would have any effect. This comes out clearly in the description of the various programmes I tried out, in the lack of success in some and in the drastic action that had to be taken in others. For instance, the contracting of all the arteries supplying blood to the prostate resulted in a severe infection of that organ, which I had, so to speak, to go to 'action stations' to put right. It was that sort of thing that tended to put my readers off trying the technique for themselves; the few examples of programmes to correct simple defects were not enough to encourage them to embark on something that might land them in a worse condition than they were in before.

I have tried to make this book a 'primer' of this method of self-healing so that anyone can understand it and apply its techniques. I hope it will result in many more people finding out that they *can* heal themselves and correct conditions that previously required the attention of a doctor, thus relieving that overworked fraternity of much unnecessary work.

I want each chapter to make sense and my readers, on reading them, to feel: 'Well, of course, I have always really believed that.' This use of the mind *does* work, and it doesn't need a superman to put it into practice. It is a simple demonstration of the old adage: 'Energy follows thought'.

There will necessarily be some repetition of what I had to say in the previous book; that is inevitable if I am to satisfy new readers. But, in the simpler form of these progressive lessons, it will be an effective way of emphasizing those elements of the technique that are essential to its success, as well as the thinking that is necessary to put them into effect. Where there were doubts and uncertainties before, I hope to have eliminated them in this presentation.

It is an exciting realization that, with positively directed thought, we can heal our bodies; and this is something that everyone can do.

# CHAPTER ONE
# BACKGROUND

The whole body is alive and is a totality of consciousnesses. This is made up of the individual consciousness of the atoms, cells, organs, etc., a consciousness that we find hard to imagine, but which programmes the limited functions of the unit and maintains a relationship to the whole. This relationship exists because of the fact that these little minds (little only because of the vehicle through which they are operating) together form part of the autonomic mind, the name given to that part of the subconscious mind occupied with the maintenance and repair of the physical body. The vestigial mind of the cell is not a separate piece of mind, it is simply mind as seen through the limits of the cell body, through which it is expressing the mind qualities of control and of choice, i.e. the selection of alternatives that are available to it. As an active element of the autonomic mind which is a part of the subconscious, it is already in contact with the mind which expresses itself through our being, but it is, with much else that lies in the subconscious, not within our conscious awareness.

Now it is interesting to observe that millions of years ago, the conscious activity of primitive life forms consisted of *all* the necessary actions for living, including the digestive and excretory processes. These, over a vast period of time, have sunk below the conscious level and are now carried out automatically by what we call the autonomic mind. That all the operations of the body were once consciously controlled makes it easier for us to understand that there can be no insuperable barrier between what is now conscious and what was conscious then, but is now subconscious. There is only one mind manifesting through the human being, but for convenience, one part has now been fenced off, not by an impenetrable barrier, but simply by a barrier with access and, in the case of this self-healing method, gaining access is a technique that can be learned.

If we take our vision far into the future, it is possible to see a time when the present operations of intellect will also have sunk beneath the threshold of consciousness, and the conscious mind will be occupied with intuition. All the intellectual faculties will then be as automatic as the autonomic processes now are. Conscious awareness has to be engaged in the sphere which leads on to the next expansion of consciousness; all else can and must be relegated to the care of that part of the mind which does not need conscious attention. We have so far proceeded in our evolution from control by instinct to control by intellect; the next step will be to reach out for control by intutition.

It is important for anyone who wants to try to influence the healing processes of the body to be clear that what I have been saying about the mind content of all cells in the body, their form of consciousness and the relation that this bears to the whole autonomic mind, is something that *can* be accepted as a reasonable working basis. It does not have to be a tenet of faith or a firm conviction of the existing state of affairs; it has to be a working proposition on which the creative imagination can seize. One must be working with the possible and natural; it is not magic that one is hoping for, but an expected natural result from a practical action that has reason behind it. It is not, as some have suggested, embarking on a technique of mind over matter. That process is already being handled very adequately by the autonomic mind in its business of keeping the body in a state of good health, exactly how, we do not yet know. No, it is a much simpler idea, though difficult enough to put into practice: that of finding the access to and making contact with the autonomic mind, which is itself part of the subconscious, a 'subsidiary' of the conscious mind.

The ironic part of this exercise is the fact that this contact already exists; there has never been any 'break' between the two functions. The access, which one can regard as a sort of opening, is more exactly a matter of putting one's conscious mind into the right kind of attitude and state to reveal the existing unity. Once that has been done, contact is natural and continuous.

Each healing process I call a 'programme'. This contains the instructions to the autonomic mind, or to the mind element of the cell, part, or organ to be affected, the picturing in the mind of what has to be done, and a regular breathing cycle to make the repetition of the programme proceed in a rhythmic manner. Some healing may require more than one programme of different content (e.g. healing an arthritic joint), and each programme consists of a ten minute cyclic repetition of a mental instruction and mind-picture. This is what I shall be referring to when I use the word 'programme'.

All the details of a programme (and I have been learning more about them over the past years of trying out new ideas) are designed to help the alignment of the two parts of the mind by sufficient penetration of the 'barrier' to get a message to the autonomic mind that will be strong enough to act on. If access were complete, it would only be necessary to give one order for the autonomic mind to take the hint, but with the difficulty we have in properly focussing the mind, it is necessary to repeat the instructions in order to make them effective.

The construction of a programme is based on the way in which we behave when we want the subconscious mind to take over some action so as to leave the conscious mind free to occupy itself with other matters. Such behaviour is typified in daily commonplace activities, whether it be brushing one's teeth, eating breakfast or driving the car. One hardly realizes that these actions have become almost automatic.

But there are other instances where one deliberately sets out to make certain actions automatic, such as learning to play a game, the piano, or in the performance of an efficient juggler or magician. In the last two examples, it is quite clear how this is achieved — by endless repetition until one does not have to think at all about what one is doing. I know from experience that the simplest moves of card manipulation must be practised over and over again until they can be done without looking at the fingers or being conscious of their movements. It probably will not mean much to my readers, but the single-handed top-palm of a card from a deck of cards took me at least six months of daily practice in order to reach the standard necessary to use the move in a demonstration of card magic. But anyone who plays the piano seriously will know what I am talking about. A difficult musical phrase has to be practised until one is able to play it, thinking only of the sense that is required from it, the light and shade of accent and tone, the melody notes to be selected and the rhythm, certainly not of how one note should follow another. It is in this way that one makes contact with the autonomic mind, a rather tedious method and one which we have to use simply because we are, at present, unable to conjure up the necessary mind force required to achieve the object with one instruction. But that will come.

Repetition is the method employed for breaking through the 'access barrier'. The reader will see that I have reinforced the power available to do this by three other important tools of the mind — visualization or mind-picturing, mental commands, and breathing. Details of how these 'tools' are employed are given in the following chapters, each of which forms a lesson in the various matters to be considered in building up and carrying out a programme.

We do know, of course, that the conscious mind is capable of influencing the autonomic mind. This fact is increasingly being taken into account by psychologists and doctors in treating their patients. It is now considered important enough to have been given a special name — psychosomatic medicine. In most cases, the conscious mind has a harmful effect on the body. For instance, worry and anxiety may lead to an ulcer, while temper and irritability, or simply living in an environment of friction, can lead to serious disorders such as partial paralysis and other apparently purely physical disabilities. But in contrast to this, there are many other known and accepted cases where the reverse has been true and a person with a severe physical disability has, through determination and decision, overcome it completely and achieved what had been a life's ambition of, say, becoming a ballet dancer or athlete. But these cases are, unfortunately, not as common, or not as commonly known, as the mental influence which produces poor health in one form or another. In this book, I shall be showing how it is possible to plan quite simply the cure of a great number of ills and afflictions by consciously using the method that we now handle so disastrously, without realizing what we are doing.

The cells and organs of the body need a happy background in which to live, just as we do. They do not want the residue of worrying, harmful and literally poisonous thoughts to filter down from the conscious mind and upset their routine. That is what happens when hate is allowed to flood the emotional body, or when continual friction restricts the natural performance of the cells' scheduled task. They should be granted the freedom to carry out joyously their appointed share of the body's maintenance and protection. If we do not allow our conscious minds to interfere with such adverse influences, then they will have this.

One word of warning: we must not interfere too much with what is now safely and effectively functioning below the level of consciousness. To try to control all the processes of the body would be a serious backward step. Much of what is achieved by some yogis through the practice of Hatha Yoga is undesirable. We should be content to use this technique to remind the body of the healing activity it should be carrying out, but for some reason is not, and we should discontinue our efforts before the completion of the cure, leaving the body to complete the process on its own. This can be done by tailing off the programme over a period of two or three weeks, reducing it by two or three minutes each week. One does not want to encourage a situation in which the cells of the body wait for direction from the conscious mind before taking the action they are designed to take under the normal direction of the autonomic mind.

To sum up briefly the attitude with which a self-healer should be equipped before starting out to influence the cells and organs of his body, he should:

1. Accept the fact, even if only as a working supposition, that every cell and organ of his body is controlled by mind and itself possesses consciousness of a limited kind. This consciousness is adequate to the particular function for which it is programmed in the general organization of the body's well-being.

2. Accept the fact that there is no separation of mind, but only of the vehicle through which it is manifesting. Contact between what we think of as separate parts of the mind therefore already exists. We have only to find out how to realize this contact and make use of it.

3. Accept that a simple technique of giving instructions to the autonomic mind is possible. We do this without knowing that we are doing it, usually with harmful consequences. A planned system must therefore be possible for bringing about beneficial results.

# CHAPTER TWO
# TOOLS OF THE MIND:
# RELAXATION

The mind makes use of many different facilities or 'tools'. In the next four chapters, we are going to consider, in some detail, four of these which are the principle elements in the self-healing technique. The tools are basically of two kinds, 'setting-up tools' and 'action tools'. This chapter, in dealing with relaxation, examines the first of the setting-up processes that are necessary if the mind is to be given the chance to work efficiently.

A tense body results in a tense mind, that is, a mind that is not restfully occupied in following a trend of thought, but agitatedly flitting from thought to thought, distracted by varied and disturbing stimuli from the senses, coming from internal or external sources. A relaxed body will eliminate, to a great extent, all those interruptions that stem from a body in which muscles are tensed and nerves charged.

Relaxation is a very important background for any deliberate and purposeful action to be taken by the mind. It is particularly difficult in these days to find an environment where our minds are not continually distracted by a multiplicity of impressions impinging on them, each starting a reaction which, however, never properly develops before the next arrives. We have become so used to this that now, when we think we are relaxed, we are not. Less disturbed, perhaps, but not relaxed. It is necessary to study the body in detail to check areas where tension still exists.

When one is working with the mind alone, that is, without drawing parallels with bodily functions, it is essential to put oneself in a condition where there is the least possible interference with one's mental activity. And even if one is able to find a relatively quiet spot in which to do this, there is a source of disturbance that is always with us: our own body. We are not generally very conscious of this in our normal non-concentrated state; the slight discomforts, which make us shift our position, little pricks and itchings and small and fleeting aches and pains, all these are continually just below the surface of consciousness, being excluded only by the fact that more pressing, urgent, or demanding sense impressions are continually shutting them out. But once you try to put yourself into a state of relaxation, all these minor interruptions will suddenly become apparent, having at last got a response from your consciousness, and you will be aware of these bodily messages as something quite unexpected. In fact, they will have been there all the time.

It is select relaxation that is required, releasing the energy from all parts of the body that the mind is not going to use in its intended task. In the case of a healing programme, the whole body would be relaxed completely except those cells, arteries, organs, or whatever it might be that the mind is going to instruct to do something — to increase the blood supply, to muster and instruct the scavenging cells, or whatever else it might be. These parts of the body, even if they have obeyed the relaxation instructions and have packed up working, will be called to attention as part of the healing programme.

Many of my readers will have already practised the technique of relaxation and they may be able to relax naturally with little conscious effort. But for many of us, relaxation does not come easily, and when we think we are relaxed, a quiet survey of the body will reveal areas and individual muscles, particularly in the face and neck, that are tense and demanding unnecessary energy. To supply this wasteful energy, the autonomic mind has to take action and, for the healing programme, it is essential that this busy mind is released from all action that is not absolutely essential for the continuance of the vital bodily functions.

For those who have difficulty in relaxing, the following

procedure should be found helpful. Once it has become familiar, the body will automatically take up the relaxed state when this is desired.

Before starting, it is advisable to loosen tight clothing such as collars and ties, belts, shoes, etc. Let the mind run round the body to see where there are any such restrictions. The position is not really important. One can either sit in a reclining or upright chair, or lie on a divan. The important thing is that the position should allow one to relax as completely as possible. I have done and still do my healing programmes in each of the three positions mentioned above, and I cannot say that I have a preference for one or the other.

After a few days of the full preliminary exercise, it will be found that the body will anticipate the checking action of the mind, and it will only be necessary to glance quickly over the body to see that all tension has been released. Eventually even this will not be necessary.

## Relaxation Procedure

Sit relaxed in a chair or lie on a couch. Take three slow deep breaths, counting six for the inhalation, three for the retention, six for the exhalation, and three before repeating the cycle. Breathe quietly and normally for a few seconds.

Let the mind rove over the body starting at the feet, and focus momentarily on each muscle or area where you think a muscle exists. Relax each muscle in turn, consciously withdrawing the energy and letting it become limp and floppy as a wet rag. This is not a brow furrowing, teeth clenching matter, but a calm instruction for the energy to be withdrawn. You should be able to feel the muscle letting go if it had previously been tensed.

Start with the toes, then pass to the instep, where one so frequently gets cramp. Pass over the ankle to the calf muscle, or wherever you think muscles are; it does not matter if you invent a few or miss some out! The mental message will be received throughout the body for the release of all the energy usually present in all muscles keeping them ready for instant action. This is the energy that does not get released without conscious attention.

Muscles over the stomach, back, arms, neck, must all come under the quiet scrutiny and be left with the energy drained from them. There are important muscles in the neck and round the face and jaws, the cheeks, brows and forehead, which are sometimes forgotten. All must be let go and become completely slack. It takes about a minute or so to run up the body in this way. At first, before the releasing action has become effective, that is, so that it can be felt, it is advisable to run down the body repeating the procedure in the reverse direction. Altogether, this exercise should not take more than three minutes at the most, and it should result in a relaxed body which will not occupy the mind's attention during the healing period more than is absolutely necessary.

It was demonstrated to me during the meditation training I underwent in Burma, which is recorded in *An Experiment in Mindfulness*, how troublesome the body could be when the mind was cut off from the more forceful of the impressions coming from the outside world via the senses. There came a time during the intense meditation practice when the outside world had faded from consciousness and the mind was intent on the subject of meditation. Suddenly I found bursting into the quietened mind a host of sharp itchings, prickings, and pains from all over the body. I found it very disturbing and could not understand what was happening. At the brief interview with the meditation master that afternoon I told him what I had experienced. 'Oh yes,' he said, 'that is something that always happens when progress is being made. These bodily sensations are always there, but they are normally shut out by the more forceful and pressing impressions received by the senses from the outside world. Just continue with your meditation and you will find that they will fade out. As your mind becomes more acutely focussed, it will automatically shut out all impressions and will be drawn into alignment with the essence of mind itself, resulting in enlightenment.' So I went away encouraged, and the trouble faded as he had forecast. The itchings and prickings gradually ceased.

I have digressed somewhat to describe this incident because it provides a convincing illustration of the way in which the body can interfere with a desired action of the mind. In the exercise of relaxation which I have outlined it is not, of course, necessary, in fact it is not desired that the mind should retire to a state where it is free from all connection with the body. What we want to do is to retain the maximum force for the particular part of the body where action is to be taken.

This relaxed state must be held during the whole ten minutes of a healing programme and this should not be found difficult. But if the body tends to tense up in certain places, then it is advisable to stop the programme and put the offending muscles back into a relaxed state. Except, perhaps, when starting off, and only if the beginner has not had any experience in relaxation, or is naturally rather a tense person, I do not think this is likely to happen in the short period of ten minutes. Sometimes it is possible that the position in which one is sitting or lying will result in a muscle becoming tense. This must be watched during the relaxing exercise and if it persists, give a mental instruction 'relax, relax' directed at a mind-picture of the offending muscle. Alternatively, you can hold a mind-picture of the energy tap being turned off and the flow of energy into the muscle being stopped.

Proper relaxation is an important prelude to a healing programme. The trouble is that we are unable, at present, to make full use of our mental potential and, therefore, we need to make the best possible use of that small proportion of power which is available to us. In order to do this, all the distractions that could reduce this effectiveness must be, as far as possible, eliminated. Proper relaxation will give the mind a clear field and the programme will *feel* much more effective. This 'feel' of a programme is an important indication that I shall refer to later.

It does help if the programme is carried out at the same time every day. The body is a stickler for routine; it likes habits whether they are good or bad. You will find, if you are able to do your relaxation exercise at regular times, that the body will adopt the relaxed state as soon as you are ready to start.

# CHAPTER THREE
# TOOLS OF THE MIND:
# BREATHING

Breathing is the second of the 'setting-up tools' that we have to consider if we want to bring the maximum amount of energy to bear on any mental project. What I have to say is, perhaps, a programme of perfection, and most people will not find it possible, at first, to bring the breathing so fully into co-operation with the giving of mental instructions and mind-picturing. But as familiarity with the run of the programme reaches a stage where it can be carried out without thinking about the procedure, it will be found that more and more of the details concerned with the breathing can be fitted in naturally.

It is not commonly accepted that breathing and the working of the mind are linked, but they are. Whereas we could quite easily make a casual remark like: 'Oh, I don't know' on an intake of breath, no one would consider giving an order such as: 'Get the hell out of here' in the same way. The more forceful the order, the greater the expulsion of breath, and this is clearly demonstrated by the sergeant-major's explosive commands on the parade ground.

We have to take careful account of how the breathing is carried out during a healing programme if we are to get the maximum benefit from the mind-power we are able to draw on.

The breathing cycle is divided up into four periods, each of which has its particular effect on how much energy is applied to the mental action initiated during that period. At the end of the inspiration of the breath, there is a short period of retention which is known as an 'interlude'. This is not normally perceptable when conscious attention is not directed to the breathing, but when it is, it is clear that there must be a pause between the end of the inspiration and the expansion of the chest and the beginning of the expiration, however slight it might be. But in purposeful breathing, coupled with mental activity, this period of the interlude has a special significance which is important. Similarly, after the expiration of the breath there is another interlude when the chest has ceased to contract and not yet started to expand. This interlude is of equal importance to the first. Both of these periods should be natural, that is, they should not be strained so that one becomes out of breath after a few cycles.

All breathing exercises should have a mind content if they are to be fully effective. Even if the aim of the exercise is simply to fill the lungs with health-giving air, one should see in the mind the fresh air circulating in the lungs and transferring its energy to the blood which it meets. One does not need to have a complicated picture which is physiologically accurate, one can make up one's own picture of what is actually happening.

The self-healing programme uses the breathing as the carrier and augmenter of the mental and visual activities that it is desired to carry out. It gives the programme rhythm, and this makes it both more effective and easier to follow. On the in-breath, the visual scene is set where the action is to take place, or the attention is called of those cells that are required to take action. It is like getting the actors of a film on to the set, and making ready to start work. That is the general rule, but some simple programmes, like increasing the blood supply in an artery, will start with just such a simple instruction, as no preliminary is necessary. But where a process is required, where cells have to be instructed to do something specific, the area where this action is required and the parts of the body which are involved should be included in the mental and visual instructions, given during the intake of breath. This will become clear when we start building up a programme. The period of inspiration defines the area where something has to be done and all those bodily units that will have to take part in the action. When this has been done, the action can start.

The upper interlude reinforces the instruction and the mind-picture that sets the scene and prepares the performers for the coming action. It is a quiet, still period when the mind is able to exert its authority, make sure that the cells have the message and know the place where they are needed; all this is done with a clearly defined mental picture. This period need only be a second or two, but can effectively be extended to the equivalent of a count of six or more if this can be done without discomfort. Normally, I would suggest a shortish period, at least to start with, one which causes no discomfort or quickening of the intake after the lower interlude.

Having got the area well defined (and this is not difficult if it is the seat of pain or if one has an X-ray picture of it), and the cells marshalled and ready to go, the instruction that will repair the defect is given on outbreathing. This is the follow-on to the order given on inbreathing. It is an order describing what has to be done and how. Since it is given on the expulsion of breath, it is a forceful order and gets the cells jumping to carry it out. Leave no doubt in the little minds of the cells which are now listening out, that you are in command and that the action you require them to carry out is one which they not only *can* undertake, but which is their proper function and that you are relying on them to perform it effectively. This is the attitude of mind that is required. It is not necessary to repeat any such words mentally, but that is how you should feel about the order you are giving. It is just and reasonable and it should give satisfaction to those carrying it out because it is the job for which they, and only they, are specially equipped.

This punch period of outbreathing is followed by a short interlude when the chest is held more or less empty. This must not be overdone because it is during this interlude, if prolonged beyond what is absolutely comfortable, that one can quickly get out of breath. Having given the instruction, the mind now sees it being carried out. The process required, whether it is the removal of infection, of calcified tissue, of fibrous lesions, the feeding of muscles or a broken limb, is pictured by the mind as going ahead. It does not, of course, need to be a physiologically accurate picture of what actually takes place. Each person will construct the picture according to his knowledge and his visualizing ability. In my case, when I started to experiment with this technique, my ability to visualize was practically non-existent, so that I had to resort to the medical books and then think out a simple, almost diagrammatic picture which my mind could quickly create. But after years of practice, this ability has improved considerably and I am now able to imagine the scene and hold it with very little trouble. Even if one has detailed physiological knowledge, it is not necessary to hold a completely accurate picture in the mind; what is needed is a simple working representation of what is to happen. Too much detail is likely to cloud the essential requirement. When one is actually carrying out a programme, it will become clear if the picture is too complicated or, on the other hand, if it is not describing clearly enough the action that should be taken.

To summarize then, the significance of the four breathing periods, the inhalation, upper interlude, exhalation and lower interlude is as follows:

| | |
|---|---|
| *Inbreath:* | The presentation of the scene where the action is to take place; calling the attention of the cells, muscles, arteries, capillaries etc. that are concerned in the action. |
| *Upper Interlude:* | Reinforcing the identification of the area where action is required; spreading the 'get-ready' message to all cells etc. concerned. |
| *Outbreath:* | The executive order for the action required. |
| *Lower Interlude:* | Seeing the action actually taking place and resulting in the desired effect. |

All of this can not be expected to be accomplished when one is learning the technique, but the aim should be kept in mind and it will be found that, as the procedure becomes familiar, more and more of the details described above will be incorporated into the breathing cycle. These details, at first too much to think of while carrying out a programme, are the means of making the programme more effective. It will work without them, but the more mind-power that can be brought into action, the more effective and the less time-consuming the treatment will be.

# CHAPTER FOUR
# TOOLS OF THE MIND:
# MIND-PICTURING

Mind-picturing, or 'think-see', is by far the most important tool that can, at present, be used for effective thinking. It is an 'action tool'. How we carry out all movements requiring muscular action, depends very largely on this facility, although we do not realize it. Any project that is born in the mind will become physically creative, depending on the extent to which it can be built into a detailed mind-picture.

Few of us realize how essential the act of visualization is to any bodily activity. We cannot do anything without first seeing it done in the mind. The mind first visualizes the action and then gives orders to the various muscles that are required to move the limbs concerned. If the mind does not know how to do a thing, it cannot be done. If it is necessary to experiment in order to find out, then, in the mind, the experimental action must show how the result is to be achieved. This is one of the basic rules for the mind — 'think-see'.

Because of this continual activity of mind-picturing, it is strange that the ability to create mind-pictures consciously varies so greatly between individuals. And yet we are all able to build detailed mind-pictures effortlessly when dreaming. Of course, it is not only in visualized images that the mind has the ability to create, but in the 'images' of all our senses, sound, touch, smell and taste. Because some of these senses are not

responsible for such imaging, the ability to hear a sound accurately or to smell a flower in one's imagination is not
commonly very great.

It is obvious that the ability of the artist to see pictures with
great detail and of composers to hear sounds is much above that
of the average individual. The ability to use the mind in any
particular way depends on the degree to which one is able to
create in the mind the medium in which we want to work. So it
seems that if we want to become proficient in any creative
medium, we should first practise thinking creatively in the field
in which we want to produce. This sounds too obvious to be
worth saying. Of course, one has to think of a scene one wants
to paint or of a phrase of music before it is written down. But
that is not quite what I mean. For instance, if I had been taught
first of all to hear in my mind simple intervals such as a minor
third or a fifth or any other two-note sound, and then continued
with the more complicated sounds of full chords, I would have
been able to write music with far greater facility than I did
experience when trying to do just this in a period of five months
whilst living in a peasant's farmhouse on a mountain in
Switzerland. Because I could not hear in my mind the sounds I
wanted to put down on paper, I had to fumble on the piano until
I found the right ones. It turned out to be such a laborious
method of composing that, after I had struggled through two
soliloquies and an étude, I gave up and concentrated on playing
what others had been able to create. It was a forceful indication
to me that one should start by training the mind before attempt-
ing to train the fingers.

It is possible to develop the ability to create in this way by pro-
gressing from the simple to the more complex mind-pictures,
and I suppose that the training of architects, engineers and many
other professionally skilled workers is handled in this way.

The most powerful aid we have in self-healing is the power to
create in the mind the action we want the body to carry out, and
the condition of the defective part when normality has been
restored. We shall have to use the imagination a lot in this work,
and it will be the creative imagination, which we shall be
handling as a tool, which it veritably is, a tool of the mind. If we

want to remove an infection, or fibrous or other unwanted tissue, we have to give instructions collectively to the white blood cells or to the scavenging cells as a group. Then we have to hold in the mind a representative picture of these entities (it does not matter whether it is absolutely true to life and, unless we have seen these cells under a microscope we would not be able to do that anyway). Again, if we wish to remove infection from a wound or a sore throat, we can imagine the infection as grey or yellow spots, or any other colour that we wish, provided we designate them in our minds as representing spots of infection. We have to make up a picture that will work. That is, when the cells are instructed to remove the infection, they must be seen to do just that, engulfing the spots of *bad* material and carrying them away, via the channels of the lymphatic system. Probably, the nearer the picture is to reality, the more effective the programme will be.

For the self-healer to be perfect at his job he would have to have the detailed physiological knowledge of a doctor, both of all the parts of the body and their functions, and he would also have to be a perfect visualizer. But we do not need to be that perfect to be effective and, over the past six years, I have proved to myself, without any room for doubt, that the limited degree of concentration and visualization I have, is quite sufficient to bring about the correction of defects that could, otherwise, only be dealth with by operation and the removal of the offending part. In three cases, the results were checked by specialists who knew what I was trying to do. In any case, the mind-picture has to be kept as simple as possible — the old principle of 'economy of effort' — and all extraneous parts of the body that are not essential in order for the action to take place, must be excluded. One can imagine a drawing of a motorcar, omitting everything but the ignition, being used by a mechanic who was tracing a fault in that system; to include, in the drawing, details of the cooling or fuel systems would merely complicate his job. In the same way, the picture of the body part and the action must be limited to the actors and scenery required for the task in hand.

I have written at length about the use of mind-picturing in the self-healing technique because it is essential to its success. In the next chapter, I shall be dealing with 'think-speak', the mental instructions that have to be given concurrently with 'think-see'. The trouble with 'think-speak' is that it can so easily become an automatic process as the saying of the Lord's prayer so often does. In fact, one always has to make an effort to attach thinking consciously to one's words. This is not so with 'think-see' and that is probably why this method is so dominant in getting one's instructions across.

In the programmes which I shall describe later, the essential and controlling factor of the whole procedure is always the 'think-see', and everything must be done to give the mind-picture the maximum effectiveness. The more interesting one can make it, the greater will be the focussing power of the mind. We find this in experience of doing things that we like, as opposed to those things in which we have no interest. It is much easier to concentrate on the intricacies of, say, a stamp collection in which we have a deep interest, than embroidery in which we may have none. So that there is a certain skill, in forming the mind-picture, to make it as realistic as our knowledge allows us: this also helps to build up confidence that what we want to happen is actually being done. When holding a mind-picture, it is better to direct it to the actual site in the body that you are imaging. Some people find that the picture naturally forms in front of the eyes and I have been asked whether this is the right way to visualize. It will work, of course, wherever the picture is directed, but it is better to relate it to the part of the body it is representing. This gives more force to the direction of the energy and the whole process becomes more realistic.

The whole subject of making use of the creative imagination is one which will come increasingly to the fore in coming years. It is a tool which we have used only subconsciously in the past, but now, in the guise of the 'as if' principle, it is being seen to have tremendous power in the creation of what we want.

# CHAPTER FIVE
# TOOLS OF THE MIND:
# MENTAL INSTRUCTIONS

In the last chapter, I dealt with 'think-see' and stressed the importance of mind-picturing in the self-healing programme. Now we have to consider the mental instruction or 'think-speak' that has to be given to the cells or whatever part of the body is required to take action. This is, of course, an 'action' tool of the mind, and is certainly accepted as such more readily than 'think-see'. However, the self-healer must be in no doubt that 'think-see' is the more important in channelling mind-power to its objective. I have already pointed out the disadvantage of this use of mind-power, when, all too frequently and easily, the mind becomes disassociated from the words and the energy that should be there is dissipated. Needless to say, the words of instruction used during a programme must have the mind fully behind them. It must not be allowed to wander off distractedly on other tracks. This is a matter of maintaining the focus and, when it is found to have shifted, of bringing it back gently and firmly to where it was directed. Do not be impatient about this if it happens, at first, too frequently. It has become a habit of mind to do this, but if it is simply brought back whenever it strays, gradually it will take the hint and the focus will be maintained with little interruption.

There is no cause for impatience or despondency at one's lack of ability to hold the mind steady behind the words; none of us normal mortals has yet perfect mind control, so that the mind will always tend to stray. The way to handle this difficulty is simply to bring it back as soon as the straying has been detected, putting the subject that caused the straying into a pigeon-hole marked 'unwanted' and categorized as 'planning', 'remembering', 'worrying' etc. But if the mind-picture is made interesting enough and the words clearly relate to what is being done in the picture, then there should be little difficulty in keeping the mind on the sense of the words for the short period of the inhalation or exhalation, continued for the ten minutes of the programme.

The words to be used should be selected with some care, but this is not difficult. Over the six years of experience with this technique, I have had to alter very little, and most of the alterations I have made have been more to suit my personal preference than to correct inaccuracies.

Let me give you an example of how to construct a simple instruction. Suppose one wants to increase the amount of blood flowing to any part of the body (and this is quite a general requirement for most healing programmes), the simplest way of giving the order is to say mentally: 'Increase blood supply to —', and here name the part of the body which has to receive the increased supply. Of course, there is a mind-picture attached to this instruction and this will be explained later when I am dealing with specific programmes. If it is desired to alert the scavenging cells (another frequent requirement) to remove infection, calcified tissue which builds up in an arthritic joint, the fibrous tissue that so often gives trouble in muscles and tendons, or any other unwanted debris from diseased or damaged parts, I find the words: 'Attention phagocytic cells', are quite satisfactory. The reason the word 'phagocytic' is used instead of 'white blood cells', which are the more numerous cells, will be explained in the chapter dealing with the removal of infection and unwanted tissue.

As well as describing briefly the mind-picture which is to accompany the instruction, the words have to be fitted naturally into the breathing cycle. One must not be too long-winded. Suppose the inhalation occupies two seconds (it will usually be just under that), then it would be wrong to try to fit into this period: 'Seek out, clear away, and destroy invading germs'. 'Seek out and clear away', or, better still, simply: 'Clear away', would fit in well. The longer phrase would probably upset the rhythm of the breathing cycle. This rhythm of the whole cycle of in- and outbreathing, 'think-speak', and 'think-see', is an important factor in the success of the programme. The three tools which are adding force to the mental action must be blended together to make a smooth-flowing, continuous process. This not only makes a programme more effective, it makes it easier.

There may well be occasions when a rather longer sentence is necessary to describe some action that is unusual or complex. I found this when I was trying, as an experiment, to teach a vein to pump, so as to lift excess blood from the prostatic venous plexus, since this excess blood was resulting in the discharge of blood with the urine. In order to accommodate the longer sentence, I had to take a slightly longer breath, longer and somewhat slower, and, once I had got used to this, there was no difficulty. The programme was eventually completely successful, but it was rather an ambitious thing to try and I would not advise anyone to embark on experiments of that kind without knowing a good deal more about the way the body works than I did!

Fortunately, there are natural safeguards which protect important organs, arteries, etc., from being interfered with by a programme that could, if effective, do a lot of harm. I found this out on more than one occasion. The first was when I tried to instruct the pituitary gland to increase the secretion of anti-diuretic hormone during the night, so as to reduce the production of urine. I kept the programme going for four months, but it had absolutely no effect. Another time, I tried to reduce the flow of blood through the kidneys at night, again in order to reduce the production of urine. Before I did this, I asked my urologist what would happen if I overdid it. He said: 'Your ankles would swell up'. I thought that would be a good enough indication that something was happening, and sufficient warning to stop the programme. But, as it happened, there was no effect at all, and after three months I stopped the programme. It is clear that important and controlling glands, as well as important arteries are much more difficult to influence with the conscious mind. Of course, it can be done, but it needs much more mental power than I am able to command. No doubt, a trained yogi would have no difficulty.

These important organs are already receiving mental instructions in the form of briefing for their job from the autonomic mind, and it is clear that the instructions given to these organs have more mind- force behind them than, for instance, instructions to capillaries, which are comparatively easy to influence. I just managed to contract the arteries supplying the prostate (though I'm not sure that this was a very good thing to do), but I got into trouble with the cell debris which resulted and which built up into a nasty infection. This had to be dealt with by calling on the scavenging cells. It was, I think, a good example of being too ambitious. Contracting arteries, other than capillaries, should always be looked at very carefully before deciding to go ahead with a programme.

It is the autonomic mind that holds the functioning programmes of all the atoms, cells, organs, and parts of the body. These should remain constant throughout life, but unfortunately they are interferred with by persistent mental energy in the form of worry and anxiety, hate, impatience, irritation etc. on the adverse side, and love, serenity, harmlessness on the good side. As the body ages, these mental programmes tend to become weaker, as do, frequently, the conscious mental processes (particularly in the field of memory), of old persons, and things start going wrong. Wherever there has been a weakness through wrong living, inheritance, or disease, the effect will be more pronounced and may lead to serious deterioration and death. This is a natural process at present. It may not be in the future, when inheritance will be controlled and living conditions purified both from the environmental angle and by personal behaviour. Then it may well be possible to continue with a healthy, fully-functioning body until such time as the resident knows and decides that it is time to leave for other fields of activity. Dying will then be a positive conscious choice.

One of the things one has to be clear about in deciding on the instruction to be given, is that it must be something that the body can carry out. It may not be something the body normally does, but it must be within its capability. Occasionally, it may be necessary to ask advice from a friendly (and broadminded) doctor in order to confirm that a planned action is in conformity with the natural function of the part of the body you are instructing. For instance, at one time, I was uncertain whether the capillaries had muscles which I could order to contract to block the blood supply to a polyp. If they had not, the order would have been a nonsense as far as the capillaries were concerned. Fortunately, it was discovered, after some research, that they had, and the programme had the desired result. One has to exercise tact, because quite a number of repairs that can be carried out by this technique of mental healing would not be accepted by many doctors. For instance, the removal of calcified tissue, and fibrous tissue, two common types of impeding deposits that occur in the body. But they do sometimes regress, and if that is so the body must have some means of bringing the regression about. Wherever there may have been a regression — even of cancer — there is an indication that some natural process of the body can be called into action, if one only knew what it was and how to initiate it.

'Think-speak' is the initiator of action, both preparatory and in the healing process. It brings 'think-see' into being and the two together form the channel, along which mental energy is sent to the cells or part of the body that is required to take action. The scene, that is the place where the action has to occur, is mind-pictured. There is no necessity to describe it in 'think-speak'. When you have decided what mental instruction you are going to give, make sure that it fits in with the mind-picture and that the two, so to speak, reinforce one another. It is this team of 'think-speak' and 'think-see' that does the work. The actual words you use are not significant as long as they are tied in with the picture. For instance, you can equally well use the words 'phagocytic cells' or 'scavengers', and all the words I will be suggesting in the sample programmes can be replaced by any you may prefer, provided that they represent what your mind is seeing.

# CHAPTER SIX
# MAKING UP A PROGRAMME

In this chapter, I shall describe how to combine the four tools of the mind to make up a programme. This is not difficult, but care is required to ensure that it is the *right* action for which instructions are being given, that is, an action that can put the trouble right and that the body is able to carry out. The 'think-speak' and 'think-see' should be simple and direct.

The first thing to do if you have a problem that you feel you want to tackle by using the mind in this way, is to get a diagnosis, unless you are absolutely sure that you know what the trouble is without one. There are many ills that will not need a diagnosis, such as a sore throat (though, of course, this might be a prelude to something more serious), a bad cut, a strained muscle etc., but for anything beyond simple damage you should have a professional opinion. From what the doctor tells you and from the lessons in this book, you will be able to decide what sort of mental instruction must be given in order to encourage the body to put matters right.

For the purpose of describing how a programme is built up, I am going to take the case of a polyp in the nose. There are two reasons for this. First, it is a programme with which I have had a lot of experience and it is a simple and straight-forward one with an easy mind-picture. The second reason is that polyps (strictly polypi) in various places in the body are fairly common. They appear in the nose, the vagina or the womb, the bladder and probably other places as well. At present, there is no cure for them but surgery, and this will not prevent them from recurring. It may well be possible, when there has been more experience with this method of self-healing, to tackle other tumours, for that is what a polyp is, a miniature tumour of a special kind, using the same programme.

A polyp is vulnerable because it hangs from a narrow neck through which pass all the small blood vessels, the capillaries, that supply it with blood. If these remain intact, the polyp will go on increasing in size. It is rather like a small balloon with the part you put in your mouth to blow it up containing the capillaries.

There may be some polyps and certainly many tumours which have a peripheral capillary supply and no vulnerable neck in which capillaries are concentrated. The capillaries will enter the polyp at points all round the circumference, wherever a supply through the adjoining tissue is available. Such a polyp is a little more difficult to deal with because the mind-picture is more complicated. I will describe a programme for dealing with this variation in Chapter 9, Programme 14.

It is quite safe to decide on a programme of contracting the capilliaries in the neck of the polyp and thus cut off the supply of blood when it is in the nose, or in any place where there is an exit for the debris that will result from its disintegration. If the polyp or small tumour were in a confined space where no exit existed, there would be a danger of infection developing as the cells were starved out and debris accumulated. In this case, a programme of 'scavenging' (see Chapter 8) would have to be started and kept going in conjunction with the contracting programme. But with a nose polyp, there is no problem.

The instruction to the capillaries to contract is, in fact, a message to the muscles by which they are surrounded, in the same way that we give an instruction to the muscles of an arm and the fingers when we want to open a door. Only in this case we give it consciously: 'Contract capillaries'. Some of us are able to waggle our ears by moving muscles at the back of the ear. To do this, we have to *feel* the muscle moving. When giving the instruction: 'Contract capillaries', try to feel these muscles around the neck of the polyp actually doing so. Use the creative imagination to do this. You will know exactly where the polyp is because the doctor or the Ear, Nose and Throat (ENT) specialist will have told you when he examined your nose. If you are doing the programme effectively, you will probably begin to feel the muscles in the neck of the polyp after a few minutes, perhaps not during the first few programmes, but when it has become familiar and is going well; there should be an aching feeling at the spot where you are seeing the polyp in your mind-picture. In order to ensure that the mind-picture is focussed on the right spot, it helps to press the finger nail firmly on the outside of the nose immediately above the place where your ENT specialist has told you the polyp is situated.

The 'think-see' needed to accompany this instruction is that of the narrow neck of the polyp from which it hangs down and blocks the free passage of air through the nostril. As you say mentally: 'Contract cappillaries', see the capillaries in the neck contracting so that no blood can flow through them. Hold them contracted in this way during the interlude after breathing in. When breathing out, the instruction will be: 'Cut off blood supply', and when you say this mentally, 'see' the narrow neck of the polyp pinched in tightly so that nothing can pass through. The breathing-in mind-picture is almost an internal view of the muscles contracting, whereas the breathing-out picture is a more distant view of the contracted neck, completely obstructing any flow of blood. These are comparatively easy pictures to hold in the mind.

The think-see pictures should, if possible, be connected like the scenes in a film and not be a succession of separate pictures. The action taken by the cells should be seen as a continuing process. Everybody has a different capacity for this technique and some may find it difficult at first. But practice will overcome this.

The complete programme, then, looks like this:

1. *To Remove a Polyp*

IN          *Think-speak:* 'Contract capillaries — tight'.

|  | *Think-see:* See and feel the capillaries contracting so as to prevent the flow of blood. |
|---|---|
| Interlude | Continue and intensify the mind-picture. |
| OUT | *Think-speak:* 'Cut off blood supply'. |
|  | *Think-see:* See the neck, as from a little distance, pinched in so that no blood can pass. |
| Interlude | Continue and intensify the mind-picture. |

All programmes are made up in this way. The small variations will become apparent when I explain other simple programmes in later chapters. Sometimes the interlude after expiration is used to 'see' the desired condition when healing has taken place. This is giving the action cells a 'preview' of what is required of them. Do not forget that in your work you are dealing with mind, primitive and elementary it may be, but it is still 'mind' with the same kind of reaction as yours, but much more limited. It is capable of being impressed by your mind. You are able to impress these small expressions of mind both by your mental attitude and by the specific mental and visual instructions.

In most programmes, but not in the one I have just described, the inhalation period is a preparative one in which a 'get ready' instruction is given to the cells, muscles, etc. that are required to take action. I use the word 'attention' for this, but any word or words with similar meaning for which the self-healer may have preference can be used equally well. The call: 'Attention phagocytic cells' will make all these cells in the affected area prick up their mental 'ears' and be ready for further instructions. One can picture swarms of these white cells mustered and waiting for action. Then when they get the executive order during the exhalation, they jump into action with alacrity. The exhalation should always have an executive significance and, whenever possible, order the main action that has to be taken.

Remember, each time before you carry out a programme or a series of consecutive programmes, to go through the relaxing exercise with deep attention to each part of the body that you are 'seeing'. The whole success of a programme depends on as little interference from the body as possible. You will find that the depth of relaxation will increase with practice, and gradually, it will be assumed automatically as soon as you sit or lie down to begin your programme. When this happens, you can omit the preliminary exercise.

For the beginner, probably one programme is enough. When I started trying out the technique, because I was tackling two complex, difficult and urgent situations, I had to do six consecutive programmes lasting, in all, an hour. But that is really too much and, except in an emergency, I would not recommend undertaking more than a couple of programmes until familiarity with the procedure has been achieved.

When starting off a programme, do not bother about *all* the details given in Chapters 5, 6 and 7. These are described in order that a programme can be made as effective as possible. Include what you can, and when the programme has become familiar, refer to these chapters and see where you can make improvements and intensify the power of your thought, but only add the improvements when this can be done naturally, without disturbing the rhythm of the programme. Too much attention to how the programme is to be carried out will detract from the direction of mental energy which is what the programme is intended to do.

If, at first, you find difficulty with the mind-picture, as I did, there are some aids you can make use of. An X-ray picture will give great assistance, particularly in cases of teeth, broken bones, or developing arthritis. There must be many others of which I have not had experience. Sometimes it is possible and advisable to substitute for the mind-picture, the feeling of pain, and direct the mental energy to this. This is simply another kind of mental creativity in the form of 'think-feel'. You will remember that, earlier, I said that any of the senses could be included under this creative vision, 'think-feel', 'think-smell' etc. There is just one word of warning about deciding to direct mental energy to the site of the pain. You have to be certain that it is not referred pain'. There are frequently times when the route taken by the nerves fools the brain into placing the sensation of pain in the wrong place. If you suspect that may be happening — your doctor should be able to tell you — then it is better to rely on a mind-picture.

The whole programme should proceed smoothly and rhythmically without any physical effort, the main emphasis throughout being given to the mind-picture. One breathing cycle will occupy from fifteen to twenty seconds and this, repeated for ten minutes, gives about forty complete breathing cycles to a programme.

# CHAPTER SEVEN
# INCREASING THE BLOOD SUPPLY

Increasing the blood supply is frequently the first requirement for self-healing. It is a function which the body is performing all the time in most of its arteries. Whenever extra work is being done by some part of the body, additional blood must be sent to it, and when it is resting again, this must be reduced.

The simplest healing programme for many of the common ills is one of increasing the blood supply. Of course, this must not be done when there is already too much blood being supplied, as in cases of inflammation; in such a case the self-healer must programme an increase of the phagocytic cells to carry away the infection.

The programme to increase the blood supply is carried out as follows:

2. *To increase the Blood Supply*

IN             *Think-speak:* 'Increase blood supply'.
               *Think-see:* See the arteries supplying the place where healing is required, having expanded to let more blood pass through.

Interlude      Continue and intensify the mind-picture.

OUT            *Think-speak:* 'Feed and build up muscle or tendon, cut, wound, or break (in a limb) or whatever you are aiming to heal.

*Think-see:* See the blood pouring through the capillaries (the small arteries which feed the various tissues in the body and the organs) at the part you wish to heal.

Interlude    Continue and intensify the mind-picture.

*Note:*    Although it feels more natural at first to increase the blood supply in the arteries on breathing out, it is necessary, in this programme, to do so on breathing in. After some practice, the slight feeling of inappropriateness will be overcome.

Sometimes, but not always, the additional blood can be felt as a warm flush in the part where the artery is being expanded. But do not be disappointed if this does not happen. If you have given the instruction, the artery will be doing its part.

As a preliminary exercise to many healing programmes, this increase of the blood supply ensures an adequate number of red blood cells carrying the nutrient to build up tissue of all kinds, as well as the blood platelets necessary for the clotting process that prevents undue loss of blood in cases of damage. It will also provide the white blood cells to carry out the scavenging of all dead and damaged tissue, foreign bodies that may have entered a wound, and any infection that may be threatening. Seeing the blood pouring into the area that is being healed will mean that back-up supplies are available to be called on if necessary.

As a preliminary programme, it is generally sufficient to do a five minute period, followed by the main healing programme. It may sometimes have to be used as a main healing programme. For instance, if you are not sure how healing should take place and have been unable to get help on the matter from a doctor, either because he does not know, or feels that you should not be 'monkeying about' with yourself in this way, then the increase of the blood supply, coupled with an instruction to heal can be an effective treatment. In this case, you leave it to the autonomic mind to do the right thing and simply make sure that the necessary supplies are kept flowing.

The programme would look like this:

### 3. *To Promote General Healing*

IN          *Think-speak:* 'Increase blood supply'.
            *Think-see:* See the enlarged arteries with more blood flowing through them.

Interlude   Continue and intensify the mind-picture.

OUT         *Think-speak:* 'Heal'.
            *Think-see:* See the blood flowing into and around the affected part.

Interlude   Continue and intensify the mind-picture.

This is a very helpful and commonly required programme for all sorts of minor ills. It is simple, with an easy mind-picture so that it would be an excellent programme to start on for one who has not tried the technique before. It avoids the necessity of finding out how the healing should actually be carried out by the body and assumes (in most cases quite correctly) that it already knows how to put matters right.

It is when, for one reason or another (and there are many possibilities), the body has been overwhelmed by a hurt, a defect, or a disease, or, because of interference, is being slack in taking the action it should, that instruction has to be given for the detailed healing procedure. This sort of situation is evident in, say, a steadily worsening arthritic condition, or something like a frozen shoulder that does not get better. These are cases where positive specific instructions are needed to get the healing process going. In simpler cases, where steady deterioration is not the problem, the increase of the blood supply, coupled with the instruction 'Heal' will add to the mental drive under which the various cells are being programmed by the autonomic mind, and result in quicker healing.

This is a programme anyone can do which should quickly demonstrate its effectiveness and, in so doing, probably surprise the person trying it out that his mind really can work miracles like this. Of course, the mind is doing this all the time, but we do not stop to think how the body is controlled consciously and unconsciously. It is a programme which can very usefully be carried out after any physiotherapy treatment that a patient is receiving. After exercising limbs or muscles, it is beneficial for the exerciser to sit for twenty breathing cycles — less than five minutes — of increasing the blood flow and building up muscles, tendons, ligaments, or whatever the physiotherapy is aiming to improve.

The same, of course, applies to any kind of exercise done on one's own, either with or without apparatus. A short period should be spent afterwards increasing the blood supply to the part that has been exercised. Again, a twenty cycle period is enough for this.

Here is a programme to build up the muscles of a limb, say after an operation; in this case, attention is directed to the quadriceps muscles of the right thigh.

## 4. To Build Up Muscles

| | |
|---|---|
| IN | *Think-speak:* 'Increase blood supply'.<br>*Think-see:* See the artery supplying the thigh expanding and sending more blood down to the muscles. |
| Interlude | Continue and intensify the mind-picture. |
| OUT | *Think-speak:* 'Feed and build up muscles'.<br>*Think-see:* See the capillaries feeding these muscles in turn by pouring blood into the muscle fibres. First let the focus rest on the rectus femoris, the large muscle on top of the thigh, then the vastus lateralis and vastus medialis, the muscles on each side, and lastly the vastus intermedius, lower down and slightly on the inside of the thigh. |
| Interlude | Continue and intensify the mind-picture. Go round the muscles again filling them with blood. |

# CHAPTER EIGHT
# SCAVENGING

Another programme that is very commonly required is one which activates the scavenging cells of the body. These are principally the white blood cells which flow round the body with the bloodstream. But there are others which are dispersed throughout the tissues, and which have the important function of removing the heavy stuff, which is beyond the capability of the smaller white cells. These have various names, but are known collectively as phagocytic cells, and this term includes the white blood cells also. Together they constitute the main defences of the body against infection and invasion by all kinds of foreign bodies (including, unfortunately, transplants).

All these cells have roughly the same action. By changing their shape, they engulf the infection or the invader and carry it away via the lymphatic system. In the kind of healing that the individual can undertake, these cells will remove infection on being instructed to do so. They will also remove the calcified tissue that forms in joints when the cartilage breaks down, as well as in the discs between the vertebrae, and from other places in the body where 'post-operative arthritis' has developed. Another useful function of these cells is in removing the fibrous tissue that causes restriction and pain in many parts of the body; this is particularly so in middle- and old age. Often, the fibrous tissue is formed as a protection or support when some part is

failing. For instance, if an important muscle has seriously deter-
iorated, perhaps because a joint is not functioning properly, the
body will form fibrous tissue in the muscle in order to hold it
together. Then, if one extends the muscle beyond certain limits,
the fibrous strings will be stretched and pain will result. Now if
the problem with the joint is put right and the muscle then built
up by physiotherapy to its former strength, the fibrous strands
will remain and still cause pain when the muscle is used. A
scavenging programme then has to be carried out to remove this
tissue which is now redundant and unwanted. This is a job for
the phagocytic cells and, although a tough one, it *is* one that they
can and will do when suitably instructed.

The less urgent and less tough scavenging can be done quite
suitably by the white blood cells, and it is therefore only
necessary to increase the blood supply to the spot where the
scavenging is required. Such a case might be a slightly infected
cut or wound, or if there is only slight evidence of fibrous tissue
in a muscle or in the sheath of a tendon (which is probably one of
the causes of 'frozen shoulder'). But where the condition is more
serious, it is necessary to call in the larger phagocytic cells to
assist the white blood cells already being supplied in the blood
circulation.

This programme of getting the scavenging cells on the job is
the next most important programme to that of increasing the
blood supply, and once one has decided how to form the mind-
picture of the cells actually engulfing the infection, fibrous
tissue, debris, or whatever it might be, it is simple and effective.
But the picture must be complete. It must show the intruder
actually being engulfed and removed by the phagocytic cell.
There is no need, however, to follow the removal along the
lymph vessels to the nodes where they are broken down. There
are so many conditions where this programme can be usefully
employed and I am sure that with further experience by those
readers who find that they can make this technique work, the
scope of the programme will be very much extended.

I have used the programme successfully to relieve the
symptoms of a 'frozen shoulder'. In this situation, it is probable
that fibrous strings form in the sheath in which the tendons slide,

making a connection between tendon and sheath which results in pain when the tendon is stretched. These string-like fibres have to be removed and it is necessary to call on the phagocytic cells to do this. I will give a programme later in this chapter that will cover the general case of removal of fibrous tissue. This tissue also forms at the neck of the bladder, particularly in association with an enlarged prostate, and can seriously interfere with the opening of the neck in order to urinate. The word 'fibrocitis' must be familiar to most of my readers. This is a condition where these fibrous threads have built up in a muscle, usually in groups or bundles, and it can be very painful. All these conditions can be overcome by a suitable scavenging programme by the phagocytic cells. But it must be persisted with because the fibrous tissue is a tough substance. I believe certain deep vibrations can be given that will help to break them up; that would certainly be a help as, in the bundle form, they take time to eliminate.

The scavenging system is normally reluctant to remove anything that the cells react to as 'home grown'. It is the reverse of this when the body decides to reject a transplant which, as far as they are concerned, is labelled 'foreign' and therefore to be ejected. If you are trying to remove fibrous tissue, it improves the chances of your doing so if you hold a background image of this tissue as harmful, redundant, and unwanted, while the programme is being carried out. As I have said earlier, they were probably formed, in the first place, to protect and support a failing muscle or weakened tendon and therefore must have been welcomed by the body at that time; but once one has been able to build up the muscle and strengthen the tendon, then the fibrous strands become redundant, and the scavengers should be told so in no mean terms. This attitude of mind will ensure that the phagocytic cells can overcome their reluctance to removing what have become intruders.

A programme to remove fibrous tissue from, say, the main quadriceps muscle — the rectus femoris — of the thigh, would be the same for fibrous tissue anywhere, but the mind-picture would, of course, depend on the location. Here it is:

5. *To Remove Fibrous Tissue*

IN              *Think-speak:* 'Attention phagocytic cells'.

                *Think-see:* See these white cells of varying sizes clustered together at the site where the pain or the thickening of the muscle can be felt.

Interlude       Continue and intensify the mind-picture.

OUT             *Think-speak:* Clear away *harmful* fibrous lesions.

                *Think-see:* See the phagocytic cells engulfing the strands of the fibrous tissue and carrying them away.

Interlude       Continue and intensify the mind-picture.

And here is a programme for the removal of infection from a cut or wound:

6. *To Remove Infection From a Wound*

IN              *Think-speak:* 'Increase blood supply' (if infection is only slight).

                'Attention phagocytic cells' (if infection is severe).

                *Think-see:* See the group of white cells and the larger phagocytic cells gathering round the site of the cut, either located by the pain or by a mind-picture.

Interlude       Continue and intensify the mind-picture.

OUT             *Think-speak:* 'Clear away infection'.

                *Think-see:* See the cells attaching themselves to the spots of infection, seen as black, grey, or yellow, and carrying them away.

Interlude       Continue and intensify the mind-picture.

And finally, here is a programme to remove calcified tissue that has formed round the site of a break in the leg, very often referred to as 'post-operative arthritis'. The site is half way down the right leg and can be visualized easily by reference to the X-ray picture taken at the time of the break.

### 7. To Remove Calcified Tissue

IN          *Think-speak:* 'Attention phagocytic cells .
                 *Think-see:* See these white cells gathering round the site of the break.

Interlude     Continue and intensify the mind-picture.

OUT       *Think-speak:* 'Clear away harmful calcified tissue'.
                 *Think-see:* See the white cells engulfing bits of the calcified tissue, i.e. little bits of bone-like substance, and carrying them away. There will be swarms of these cells but they can only take away very small bits at a time.

Interlude     Continue and intensify the mind-picture.

If Programme 7 is required to remove the calcified tissue forming in a joint, a mind-picture of the joint is necessary, indicating just where the cartilage has broken down and the hardened tissue formed. If there is an X-ray picture, it can be created from that, but if not, then reference should be made to a medical book such as *Gray's Anatomy* (in the 35th or later edition) where a suitable picture of the joint will be found. The mind-picture then has to focus on the position or positions where the calcified tissue is seen to have formed, or, if without an X-ray, where the main wear and tear is located in the joint. Sometimes the spot can be located accurately by the pain felt.

In some cases, fibrous tissue will have formed in two muscles of the thigh or, in the case of an arthritic condition, calcified tissue will be present in different parts of the joint; for example, where the hip is affected, there will be formations of this hardened tissue, both on the head of the femur and in the acetabulum (the socket). In these cases, do not attempt to visualize the separate places where action by the cells has to take place at the same time, but let the mind-picture focus first on one spot and then on the other. This is done in the same way as you would move a torch light to illuminate different areas of a darkened room. Trying to hold the various sites in the picture together has the effect of lessening the mental power that is directed to each one.

The reader will find many other cases where a scavenging programme is indicated, and he should have no difficulty in making up his own programme, after the models given in Programmes 5, 6 and 7, to suit his particular condition.

# CHAPTER NINE
# SOME USEFUL PROGRAMMES

In the earlier chapters, I have outlined seven programmes that heal, either by increasing the blood supply or by carrying away harmful foreign invaders. From these simple basic programmes, others can be constructed. I am giving in this book only those programmes with which I have had experience and success. It is true that, in some cases, I cannot definitely say that the improvement or removal of the condition was solely or even partly brought about by the programme, because other treatment was being followed at the same time. But, whereas previously the orthodox treatment was not having any effect, when the programme was added to it, there was improvement within two or three weeks. This applied to two cases of seriously reduced blood platelets, one in London and the other in San Francisco. In the latter case, I was trying out the possibility of distant treatment with little or no contact. In the London case, I had regular contact by telephone. The programme is a fairly simple one and I will include it in this chapter. It was because it was simple and 'felt' right that I was confident it would have some effect. But I cannot really say that it had anything to do with the improvement which followed in both cases. Since these cases, I have not tried any more distant healing, and I will discuss this aspect in a later chapter.

The first programme I want to describe is one that can be very useful, and it deals with a condition for which I understand there is no remedy other than dental surgery. It was one of my earliest successes and concerned infection in the root canals of three teeth. If this is shown up on an X-ray, there is little that can be done about it except hope that it will clear up. If it does not, it will eventually cause trouble and pain and the affected tooth will have to come out.

The programme to deal with this is given below. It is assumed that the self-healer will have seen the X-ray and will therefore be able to create a simple mind-picture of the infected area.

### 8. *To Remove Infection From the Root Canal of a Tooth*

IN              *Think-speak:* 'Attention phagocytic cells'.
                *Think-see:* See these cells penetrating the bone of the root of the tooth and collecting in the canal round the area of infection.

Interlude       Continue and intensify the mind-picture.

OUT             *Think-speak:* 'Clear away infection'.
                *Think-see:* See the spots of infection being engulfed by the phagocytic cells and taken away through the bone of the canal.

Interlude       Continue and intensify the mind-picture. Finish by seeing the canal cleared up and free from all infection.

If the infection is in the early stages, it will probably take a month of daily effective programmes to clear it up.

I mentioned in Chapter 6 that the removal of a polyp from a site where there was no natural exit (such as is present in the nose or vagina) could result in infection, caused by the debris of the starved out cells. Where this is the case, there is an alternative programme that is effective. In fact, I used this programme before I worked out what I thought would be a more effective one, that of contracting the capillaries. I have since discovered that the contracting programme sometimes does not work, and this puzzled me a great deal. I believe now that it must be because the polyp has additional sources of supply, either through some peripheral capillaries or perhaps some nutrient existing in the area and not supplied by capillaries. If a polyp proves stubborn with a contracting programme then it is best to switch to the programme given below.

### 9. To Remove a Polyp — Alternative Method

IN  *Think-speak:* 'Attention phagocytic cells'.
*Think-see:* See these cells collecting round the polyp ready for action.

Interlude  Continue and intensify the mind-picture.

OUT  *Think-speak:* 'Clear away polyp tissue'.
*Think-see:* See the phagocytic cells eating into the polyp and reducing its size.

Interlude  Continue and intensify the mind-picture. Finish by seeing the polyp having been removed altogether and the site clear.

This programme could also be tried out on a tumour, but I have had no experience of this. A tumour can be either of the polyp type being nourished through a narrow neck and therefore very vulnerable to the blood supply being stopped, or it can be supplied by peripheral capillaries. It is probable that a cancerous tumour is of this latter kind because the cancer cells have the particular ability to attract capillaries to them. I will suggest, later in this chapter, how such a tumour (but not a cancer) can be dealt with by a slightly modified mind-picture.

I come now to another simple programme that can be a valuable adjunct to the usual medicaments that soothe but do not often cure. This is a programme to heal a sore throat. But I must add a warning. A sore throat can often be the prelude to something much more serious and, in any case of doubt, a doctor's opinion should be sought.

### 10. To Relieve a Sore Throat

IN  *Think-speak:* 'Attention phagocytic cells'.
*Think-see:* See the cells gathering in the area where the throat feels sore.

Interlude  Continue and intensify the mind-picture.

OUT     *Think-speak:* 'Clear away infection'.
        *Think-see:* See the cells engulfing the spots of
        infection and carrying them away.

Interlude     Continue and intensify the mind-picture. Finish
        with a mind-picture of the throat clear of all
        infection. This is presenting the phagocytic cells
        with the target they are aiming at.

I have had experience of two cases of 'frozen shoulder', both
of which were distant healing programmes. In both cases the
condition cleared up, but whether this was due to the programme, I can not say. There are so many instances where a
condition regresses to the normal healthy state without any
medical attention and even some that regress when a cure has
been stated to be unlikely, that it is always difficult to rule out an
improvement as a simple case of regression. However, I would
be satisfied if it turned out that this kind of self-treatment
resulted in more instances of regression than could possibly be
expected.

Although I do not think it is yet known for certain what
exactly causes a 'frozen shoulder', if indeed it is not a term used
to describe a variety of painful conditions, I took it to be the
formation of fibrous lesions between the tendon and the sheath
by which it is surrounded. These strands of fibrous tissue bind
the tendon to the sheath, so that when it is stretched, pain is felt,
and it can be acute.

The programme to deal with this condition is given below.

11. *To Relieve a Frozen Shoulder*

IN     *Think-speak:* 'Attention phagocytic cells'.
        *Think-see:* See these cells collecting inside the
        tendon where the pain is felt.

Interlude     Continue and intensify the mind-picture.

OUT     *Think-speak:* 'Clear away fibrous lesions'.
        *Think-see:* See the phagocytic cells attacking the
        fibrous strands which bind the tendon to the
        sheath, and see them being carried away bit by
        bit.

Interlude    Continue and intensify the mind-picture. Finish by seeing the tendon able to move within the sheath without restriction.

The problem of increasing the population of blood platelets came to me from a close friend who was suffering from a dangerously reduced count of these important cells. They are the cells which take the first action to stem the loss of blood in any tissue or part of the body. All the little bruisings, knocks etc. which the body suffers all the time would, without the action of these cells in blocking the leak from the damaged spot, result in a constant and serious loss of blood throughout the body. When the count is seriously reduced, these bruisings show up all over the body like small blood blisters. The platelets act rather like a rag stuffed into a hole in the hull of a boat to reduce the leak until such time as a proper repair can be made.

The blood platelets are produced from the bone marrow cells by a process described as hiving-off'. These offspring of the bone marrow cells then continue an independent life in the blood stream. The programme aims at increasing this hiving-off process and thus building up the population of these cells in the blood stream. The usual treatment for this condition is a drug therapy with steroids, sometimes reinforced by the removal of the spleen. It is a serious condition, and if the count is reduced below a certain level, the patient will have to be taken care of in hospital, in order to prevent the dangerous results of the kind of bruising associated with normal daily ativity.

### 12. *To Increase Blood Platelet Count*

IN    *Think-speak:* 'Attention bone marrow cells'.
*Think-see:* See these cells in the narrow channel of a bone. You do not have to picture a particular bone for this, just imagine a bone with the marrow flowing through the centre.

Interlude    Continue and intensify the mind-picture.

OUT    *Think-speak:* 'Increase production of platelets'.
*Think-see:* See little slivers of the bone marrow cells becoming detached from the main body of

the cells and proceeding on their own into the blood stream.

Interlude    Continue and intensify the mind-picture.

With this programme, if it is being carried out as a distant healing, it is helpful to have a report, at intervals, on the state of the cell count.

It is the gradual wearing away of the cartilage in a joint that leads to the depressing condition of arthritis. Sometimes it appears to be more a condition of disintegration that is taking place, but more often, it is the result of excess activity coupled with incorrect diet. The deteriorating cartilage tends to calcify into hardened tissue. This is a natural process which takes place throughout the body in the early days of infancy, when much of what is now bone tissue started as cartilage. This is, presumably, to allow the necessary flexibility of the body during birth. The cartilage in the joints, which is of a type described as hyaline articular cartilage, should not deteriorate in this way if it is properly supplied with the nutrient it requires. However, for reasons not yet known, the deterioration happens all too frequently and the resulting pain and restriction of the joint becomes progressively more serious.

If the deteriorating condition of the joint is detected early enough, it is possible, with a suitable programme, to increase the supply of nutrients and build up the cells to something like their original form. But if the deterioration has proceeded to the stage where the cartilage has formed calcified tissue, then this must first be removed by a scavenging programme making use of the phagocytic cells. The programme given below is to increase the supply of nutrient to the cartilage. This is supplied from the blood and the synovial fluid. The fluid is secreted from the synovial membrane which surrounds the joint. The nutrient is to be visualized as a colourless liquid.

13. *To Increase the Supply of Nutrient to the Cartilage*

IN          *Think-speak:* 'Increase nutriment'.
            *Think-see:* See an increased flow of clear liquid from the membrane surrounding the joint.

Interlude       Continue and intensify the mind-picture.

OUT             *Think-speak:* 'Feed and build up (or extend) cartilage'.

                *Think-see:* See the nutrient liquid flowing to the cartilage and the cartilage being extended throughout the joint.

Interlude       Continue and intensify the mind-picture. Finish by seeing the cartilaginous lining of the joint complete.

Programmes number 1 and 9 were aimed at removing a polyp by two different methods. The method of contracting the capillaries in the neck of the polyp applies to any tumour of this kind, that is, where the blood supply is through a narrow neck. It is probably more common for tumours to be supplied peripherally by small blood vessels entering over the whole circumference of the tumour. Either of the methods already given for removing a polyp can be used for removing a tumour of this kind, but a somewhat different picture is required than for a Programme 1 removal.

### 14. *To Remove a Tumour with Peripheral Blood Supply*

IN              *Think-speak:* 'Contract all capillaries'.

                *Think-see:* See all the capillaries which supply the tumour contracting where they enter the tumour. They will be entering at positions scattered all round the tumour. The muscles must be seen to be completely closing the channel through which the blood has been passing.

Interlude       Continue and intensify the mind-picture.

OUT             *Think-speak:* 'Cut off blood supply to polyp'.

                *Think-see:* See all the capillaries surrounding the polyp pinched in and completely blocking the passage of blood.

Interlude       Continue and intensify the mind-picture.

If this tumour is in a location where removal of the debris might cause difficulty and result in infection and inflammation, a programme of scavenging would have to be carried out, following on the ten minute programme outlined above. It may not be necessary, but the possibility of an unpleasant and painful result is not worth risking.

I have had an instance, when working on a polyp in my nose, of the complete failure to produce any effect after two months of a regular programme of contracting the capillaries. I came to the conclusion that the polyp was being supplied either by some peripheral attachment or through the environment, as discussed earlier. I had to switch to the scavenging programme, and this has the desired result. This brings out the important point that if a programme fails to produce the desired effect when it 'feels' satisfactory, it is much more likely to be caused by the fact that the programme itself is incorrect, that is, that it is trying to do something that the body can not do, than that the technique is faulty.

I have had other similar instances, which I have referred to earlier, notably when I tried to influence the secretion of hormones from the pituitary gland. But in that case, the body was unable to respond because the original direction from the autonomic mind was too strong for me to override it with the conscious mental power I could bring to the task. On thinking it over, I came to the conclusion that this was to be expected because the pituitary gland is one of the important controlling organs of the whole body's economy. One has to realize all the time that one is not dealing in magic, but in rational response. There is always a reason for the failure of a programme; sometimes this can be overcome by a change in the instruction, but there will always be cases when it is at present beyond the capability of the mind to achieve the desired effect.

# CHAPTER TEN
# ODDS AND ENDS

During the past six or seven years, I have been limited in developing this self-healing technique by what I have been able to try out on myself and, in a few cases, on others. This has enabled me to study in the necessary detail the physiology and pathology of the affected parts of only a very limited selection of the common ills that beset the body. It is now necessary for a far greater study to be made in order to extend this technique to its legitimate boundaries, to get a better idea of its full potential and of its limitations. There are obviously many improvements to be made in the technique and for these I depend on the many readers who will have far better qualifications than I have and who will be able to devise programmes for a wide variety of ills which I have been unable to tackle.

To a newcomer starting on this technique, it may appear strange, unconvincing, and perhaps somewhat superficial. But once a programme has become familiar and the self-healer has settled down into a period of rhythmic breathing and thinking, he will get a 'feel' that it is going well. If after a week or so, it still feels strange, then something about the programme requires adjustment. With a good programme, that is, one that is obviously giving the right instructions, such as the removal of infection from a cut, there should be some evidence in a week or so. But of course, this period does depend on the ability of the self-healer to blend the elements of the programme into a smoothly flowing routine. The programme should not be a mental effort in the sense of 'getting through it at all costs'. There should be enough interest in giving the instructions and in 'seeing' them being carried out, for the mind to follow easily the sequence that has been decided on for the programme.

The time scale for the effect of a programme to become apparent is a little difficult to give with any general application. But as a rough indication, there should be some sign of effect within fourteen days of starting a simple programme. For a programme such as the removal of a polyp, more like a month is necessary. For the building up of cartilage or the scavenging of calcified tissue, probably a rather longer period would be required, but this, of course, depends on the degree of deterioration that had occurred in the joint. In my own case, when trying to relieve a severe and developing arthritis of the hip, it took me a year to eliminate completely the pain from the joint. During that time, some six weeks would be spent on removing an osteophyte, one of the small bony pinnacles that are characteristic of osteoarthritis and which cause so much acute pain. This had to be done before it was possible to start the reconstruction of the cartilaginous lining of the joint.

One has to be patient. It took the body a long time to reach the condition that you are trying to heal, and it will take a comparable time to get a regression under way and the healing completed. For that is what we are doing, encouraging the body to regress the process which has resulted in the painful state. As a corollary to this, where there has been a case of regression of no matter what kind of disease or disability, we have only to find out how that regression took place, that is, what the body did in order to repair the defect, in order to devise a programme to produce the same result consciously. There have been many remarkable and inexplicable regressions which have been recorded by doctors and specialists, demonstrating the body's as yet undiscovered abilities, and I am sure that, in time, it will be possible to initiate these with the conscious mind.

There is no doubt that the continual practice of this technique results in more mental power being transmitted to the recipient cells, muscles etc. that are being called into action by the programme. I have been carrying out programmes now, daily, for over six years, and the development of my ability to make and retain effective mind-pictures has been considerable. It should really be necessary to give the order only once for the cells to take action, as happens in the daily control of our physical movements, and I have no doubt that, as the technique is improved with much greater experience, such positive control will come about. During the next fifty years we are going to find so many ways of using the mind that would now be considered magical, that what I am writing about will be thought of as commonplace. But mind-power like atomic power and all kinds of energy is neutral. It has no natural affinity with either good or evil. It is the mind behind the power which decides that. Only when the human being has transcended the selfish separative urgings of his lower self, will the full power of the mind be revealed. Man will then step into his rightful place as the controller of his physical vehicle and the energies by which it is affected in his life on earth.

Quite a number of people, when starting out on this technique, will find that they are poor visualizers. It would be a help, and of great advantage where group therapy is being carried out, to provide pictures and perhaps even films of the various kinds of healing that certain programmes are initiating. These could be factual representations in cases which are not too complex for the creation of a simple mind-picture, or a more or less diagrammatic representation when that is indicated.

The instruction of groups of individuals, all with the same problem, was referred to by Dr Forbes in his introduction to my previous book (*Mind Your Body*) on this subject, and I am hopeful that, before long, such group self-healing sessions will be organized.

This should be a very effective way of using this technique. It would, I feel, be an important development, not only because the modern tendency is towards group work, but also because the lack of concentration or visualization ability in one of the members of the group will be offset by the formation of a 'group image'. It will be easier to build the confidence that is necessary in order to direct the mental energy to the part being treated. And working in a group stimulates one to greater effort.

The group should be formed of those having the same disease, defect, or illness, and I would think that ten or twelve should be the maximum number. The therapist, who should preferably, but not necessarily, be a doctor, should begin the course by explaining with simple diagrams what has gone wrong in allowing the body to produce the symptoms from which the group is suffering. He should then explain what the body is capable of doing to remedy the situation. This should be done with as much detail as he judges the group generally capable of making use of. Simple line diagrams should be displayed showing the action that has to take place in order to put matters right. He should then describe in detail the technique to be followed, taking each element of the programme in turn; relaxation, breathing, mental instructions and visualization, suggesting the mind-pictures and giving the mental instructions to be used during the various parts of the breathing cycle.

When all members of the group are quite clear about what they are to do and how to do it, a period of ten minutes should follow for each member to carry out the programme on his own. Before beginning this period, the therapist should take the group through a relaxation routine of his own choice, one that can be followed simply by each member when practising by himself.

On completion of the period of independent practice, the therapist should enquire what difficulties had been encountered and both explain and enlist suggestions from the group for overcoming these. Then it would probably be sound to take the group once again through the details of the programme emphasizing the points where difficulty had been met. It will probably be necessary to carry out the programme individually for a couple of sessions in order that the less quick to master the technique can catch up on those who take to it without difficulty (as many will). Depending on how the sessions are organized, I would suggest that for the first few days, two sessions a day, one morning and afternoon would be adequate. When the routine has become familiar, the sessions could be reduced to one a day. But of course, the therapist would have to decide this according to the progress that was being made.

When the group starts to follow the routine as a group, it should be pointed out that the group mind-pictures and mental instructions will form a single source of energy from which all will be drawing. This will considerably augment the effect that the programme will have on each of their bodies. They should be instructed to try to sense the group force that is adding to the power of their own minds. The benefit of any kind of group therapy is the synthesis of individual effort into a group effort, with the increased background of energy feeding back into the individual to give him a much greater ability to achieve the desired end.

These are, of course, merely my suggestions as to how group therapy should be conducted, but I have never tried it out. I am sure that there are therapists who are experienced in group treatment who could bring out the strong points of its application to this technique of self-healing, and arrange a programme of treatment easy to follow and capable of being assimilated by those with a minimum of knowledge of the various functions of the body. I would be grateful if they would let me know of their experience, where improvements have been introduced, the facility with which the programmes were followed and, of course, the results.

This brings me to the main point that stands out from my limited experience — the need to acquire and co-ordinate the experience of many individuals trying out programmes for all kinds of conditions. At present, I do not know how much detailed knowledge is necessary to produce the desired effect. I have read of systems of psychic healing which use mind-pictures to heal, but these are nearly always symbolic and need bear little or no relation to the actual process of healing that the body would have to follow. I know that this kind of symbolic picture is of no use in the technique I have been experimenting with. I tried it out over the period of a month in a programme to remove a polyp. I had thought that, if the mind-picture included a ligature being pulled tight round the neck of the polyp, completely shutting off the flow of blood, this would be more effective than just visualizing the muscles of the capillaries contracting. But in fact, nothing happened. On thinking the matter over I realized that the body had no means of getting hold of a ligature and what I was instructing it to do was a complete non-starter. If one is giving an instruction to cells or to an organ, it must be one which that particular part of the body has been programmed by the autonomic mind to undertake. But, as in most cases, one does not know exactly what the process looks like, the picture must be an imaginative one. But how imaginative or how true to life the picture of the healing process should be, I do not yet know. This is something that further experience will tell us.

As far as the technique is concerned, I have no doubts about the content of chapters 1 to 6. However, when it comes to the programmes themselves, the information I have given is based only on the experiences I myself have had. I am sure that these can be improved upon and that they will be given greater punch. One advantage of this technique of healing is that one is always trying out new variations on a very sensitive guinea-pig — oneself! I sincerely hope that those with serious complaints will not be tempted to repair them themselves without a doctor's diagnosis and assistance. It may well be that, in so doing, they will not be able to say that their own programme was responsible for the elimination of the condition, or has even helped towards it. That does not matter; what does, is that every possible aid should be brought to the healing process. One is not trying to demonstrate that the technique works, that can be shown by many other simple programmes which can safely be carried out without medical assistance.

Further progress is now dependent on the extent to which my readers can contribute their experience, and I shall make some suggestions concerning this at the end of the book.

# CHAPTER ELEVEN
# FUTURE POSSIBILITIES

In this chapter, besides describing other applications that are possible but with which I have had no success, I want to let fancy roam a bit and consider certain possibilities which are not yet within the capability of the mind but which might well be when the full reach of the mind is beginning to be realized. As I mentioned earlier, we are not indulging in 'mind over matter'; we are doing something which is much simpler once we have learned the secret — that of communicating with lesser minds.

I mentioned earlier, too, the idea of holding a mental impression of the infection you are trying to get rid of, or perhaps a polyp, as being unwanted and harmful. In this way, any reaction the cells might have, that they were being told to get rid of something that had been a useful and needed part of an organ, could be overridden. I had another example of the same thing, but one that could be much more important. A man wrote to me who had had a kidney transplant and had to remain on heavy and continuous drug therapy to prevent the body rejecting the kidney. He asked me whether I could advise him of a programme that would prevent this. I replied making a suggestion for him to try, and in his next letter, it seemed to be having some success. But unfortunately, he ran into other troubles with his heart and his breathing and was unable to continue with the self-treatment. I am sure that it is possible to feed in a strong mental impression that the kidney is friendly, despite the recognition signal the scavenging cells were receiving.

Exactly how to do this needs experimenting with. Medical science does not yet know how to prevent the rejection of transplants other than by the dangerous method of interfering with the body's defence mechanism. This, while sometimes successful, can lead to complex and undesirable drug manipulation of the natural processes of the body. The trouble is that the body's immune system is capable of recognizing a 'stranger in the house' and when it does this, has all the facilities for taking drastic action. This results in the destruction of the foreign body whether it is an infection or an implant. Now at the end of the recognition trail, the instruction to the scavenging cells is a mental one. This might have been triggered off by a chemical reaction, by some difference in the cell form, or by some other action that, at present, we do not know about. But however the fact that 'here is a foreigner' has been made known, the instruction to the cells to eject the invaders will be in the form of a 'taped' or instinctive mental reaction from the autonomic mind. It is a 'built-in' reaction for which the scavenging cells have been programmed. It is necessary, therefore, to override this mental programming which results in the rejection. This could take the form of an instruction to 'disregard' the instinctive reaction, and a positive impression that the particular group of cells they were intent on rejecting were beneficial, friendly and worthy of love rather than aggressive harmful action.

As this function of the scavenging cells is a very important one in the body's immunization system, it will be brought into action by a correspondingly strong taped instruction which appears as the automatic reaction to certain stimuli. So we have somehow (as the cancer cell manages to do) to confuse the scavengers to make them sufficiently uncertain about the nature of the 'invader' so that they do not react. The problem needs a number of different experiments with transplant patients. I believe there is sometimes a reverse situation where the transplant rejects the body; this might well turn out to be an easier case to override, and I would try to do this with a programme to beam down love at the transplant to make it feel welcome in its new habitat. In the more normal case of rejection, I hope for suggestions from my readers, and indeed, that some of them might try out on themselves ways and means of changing the minds of the scavenging cells.

The problem presents two possible courses of action; the first to persuade the scavengers that, in spite of their recognition information, the strangers are friendly, and the second, to prevent them from taking scavenging action despite their reaction to the recognition signal. I believe the first alternative is the more likely to succeed, but there may be other choices.

Let us stretch our minds a little further and look at what might be called 'replants'. The embryo has developed from a single cell. In that cell were carried the blue prints of all the parts of the body. As the original cell split into two, and then four, and continued to divide in this way, specialization began. This meant that from now on, only certain parts of the blue print were utilized for each cell according to what part of the body they were destined to form, the rest of the blue print being in some way rendered inoperative for those particular cells. The blue print is, in fact, a 'taped' mental instruction from the autonomic mind and, as the cells progress gradually into a more and more specialized and therefore restricted field, all the instructions not required fade from the cell consciousness into what we, with our advanced conscious make-up, call the sub-conscious. But there still remains, in the cell's subconscious, the potential for the production of any part of the body. Every cell throughout the body possesses this.

When a part of the body was being finished off, say an arm having arrived at the fingers, something told the cells when these were completed and the blue print then prevented the production continuing to form endless fingers. Like a knitting pattern, there was a finishing off process, rounding off the tips of the fingers and completing the nails. All this was achieved by a complex mental instruction, contained within the blue print and passed on to the various cells concerned with finger production. Now, supposing a finger is lost in an accident, all the cells in the stump still have in their subconscious the potential of building up the finger to its original form. But is it possible to bring this potential from the subconscious into conscious activity?

We know that by psycho-analysis it is possible to bring matters long submerged in the human subconscious into conscious awareness, and thereby relieve repressions that have been the cause of physical restraints and disabilities. We have, therefore, to find a method of bringing what lies in a cell's subconscious into functioning activity. I do not think this is impossible. We know that we can make a mental connection between our own conscious mind and its counterpart in the cell; we know that we can communicate with our own subconscious by making use of special techniques. It therefore does not seem to be too outrageous a suggestion that it is possible to find a way of realizing this subconscious potential for reconstituting damaged or lost limbs and organs. Of course, one would have to be careful to be precise in doing this. We do not want, for instance, to produce a bladder or a kidney at the end of a finger! We shall have to learn how to reactivate only that part of the cell's subconscious that was concerned with the original production of the finger.

This is not really a remote fancy. It is a logical progressive step from what this book is about — the contact with and control of the mind that is responsible for cell activity.

Instead of transplants then, we shall be able to put into practice the regrowth of organs and parts of the body that, for one reason or another, are failing. We must, however, take into account that, very often, the cause of the member's failure will lie in damage to the blue print, and unless we are able to correct that, the new member will be produced with the same deficiency that led to the failure of the original.

This ability, in certain species of animals, to regrow limbs and organs is well known to biologists. It seems that, as our bodies became more sophisticated, we lost this ability. Now, as our minds are becoming more sophisticated, perhaps we shall be able to recover it.

The mind is immensely powerful. It needs to be constrained and directed like a laser beam so that its energy is not dissipated.

When we can control it in this way, we shall be able to pass brief instructions that will bring instant results. We shall be able to kill off cells that are causing harm, and all the harmful invaders of our bodies, once they had been identified and, if they had not already been dealt with by the body's automatic immunization system, could be instantly dispatched. But this is, at present, a potential only, and it will be long into the future before it can be realized. Why? Because such mind-power will need to be balanced by a purity of motive that we are, at present, far from possessing. What a witch-doctor can now do to his enemies is child's play compared with the havoc a mind endowed with the control I have pictured could wreak, if it were being directed by a man with the self-centred outlook of most of humanity today. We have a long road of purification to follow before the true nature and place of mind can be realized in action.

I would now like to return to more practical future applications of this technique of self-healing. These are projects which can be undertaken by interested readers, but which I have been unable to handle myself, or have tried out and failed to produce any result.

The first of these is distant healing. I have tried this on half a dozen occasions and am really unable to say whether I was instrumental in the improvement that resulted or not. I am sure that there is no particular difficulty about this though there are certain disadvantages. In those cases that I have tried, I have proceeded exactly as in self-healing except that the mind-picture is projected to the person being healed. I found that it helped to make the necessary contact if I held in my hand during the treatment, a blood spot on a piece of blotting-paper (as is generally required in radionic treatment), a piece of hair, or a photograph. I felt a very definite lack in that I was working in the dark; I had no ability (psychic sense?) that would enable me to diagnose the trouble or to receive feedback on the progress, or lack of it, that the treatment was resulting in. This lack could be dangerous because one *might* be trying to do something that could harm the body, and one must know this at once. In the case of self-healing, one is very quickly aware of harmful results and can take the necessary action before real harm is done. In distant healing this is not the case and one cannot always rely on the person one is working on having the same degree of perception into physical reaction that one has oneself. This is a very important defect of this method, unless the healer has the necessary psychic perception to be able to 'see' for himself.

The other main drawback is the time required. For each element of treatment a ten minute period is necessary. Many treatments might require two of these so that a period of treatment for three persons could, on this basis take one hour. That is a lot of time during which this kind of concentration must be kept at its peak, and few would be prepared to undertake it. However, if the healer has the necessary psychic perception to be kept aware of the progress of the treatment, distant healing using this technique can be effective. I do not think it would be practicable to take on more than an isolated case, and probably only then when a personal connection exists. That is, of course, based on what I know about it at present, which is not much. It is probable that a particularly gifted person could cut down the time required for a programme to a few seconds of concentrated vision, in which case, healing could become a life's work just as it is with many other healers.

I want to say a few words about energy direction. Although I have had no success in the few times that I have tried this out, I am sure that it is now a possible means of hastening healing and regeneration. The trouble with a healing programme using directed energy is that the energy will be delivered both to the affected normal tissue cells and to whatever abnormality is causing the trouble. To give an example: Suppose there is a formation of fibrous tissue in a muscle of the thigh and the muscle itself has become debilitated, if one then directs energy to the muscle, one cannot prevent it being directed also to the fibrous tissue in the vicinity, which will therefore become stronger. But there would be cases, such as a broken limb, where energy direction could have a beneficial result. The energy is taken in and redirected as follows:

15. *To Take In and Direct Healing Energy*

IN          *Think-see:* See the energy (from the sun) that is all round us being drawn in at a spot between the shoulder blades and concentrated in the area of the spleen (located immediately below the left dome of the diaphragm under cover of the ribs).

OUT    *Think-see:* See the energy as a golden stream proceeding from the spleen to the spine and hence to the area that requires it, along pathways that run parallel to the nervous system.

Bear in mind always that this energy will feed the good cells and the bad, and even if there is some unknown trouble brewing in the area that you know nothing about, this additional energy may well bring the trouble to the boil.

I mentioned earlier, the need for feedback if distant healing is to be carried out safely and successfully. But it is also a definite requirement for self-healing. If one is able to make contact with the mind element of a cell (that is, a part of the autonomic mind), then the contact should be two-way. It should therefore be possible to receive back from this elementary mind the sort of information one so badly needs. This would include inform-ation about:

- the real situation
- whether the proposed treatment is possible
- whether the treatment is taking effect
- whether other effects are threatening, e.g. infection from decaying debris.

In fact, one should be able to 'read' the mind of the cell or part that one is treating, simply by virtue of the connection that has been made. I have received no information which I could definitely say was the result of feedback, though I have had rather surprising bright ideas at critical times during a treatment. But I am sure that this feature can be developed. It will obviously be easier for some, but all could, I believe, by training, become receptive in this way. What sort of training this should be, I leave to others to find out who may have the kind of perception that I so clearly lack.

It seems to me that feedback could come in either of two

ways. The first and most natural would be the two-way communication I have already referred to, and the other is in the information obtained through the psychic sense that many healers, and others who are not healers, possess. Shafica Karagulla M.D., in her book *Breakthrough to Creativity*, was surprised to find how widespread the possession of E.S.P. abilities were in the U.S.A. during a research project on the subject. A number of those with this psychic gift were doctors who, though making use of the ability for diagnosis, had kept quiet about it for fear of being regarded as quacks. They only agreed to talk about their unusual talent provided their names were not mentioned. Those who have this gift would start with a great advantage for distant healing by this mind method, but I am convinced that the direct mental feedback is a logical outcome of practising this technique.

And lastly, there is one other matter which is important, about which I have not been able to do anything; that is, dealing with nervous defects. I feel that there is a good prospect of bringing about the repair of many nervous defects which, at present, defeat medical science. These are mainly caused by interference with the passage of minute electrical currents that trigger off all our physical activities. Whether they are consciously controlled or under the control of the autonomic mind, these obstructions and interferences originate in the mind. At present, I have no idea how to tackle this problem, but I am sure that many of my readers will have opportunities to try out various approaches. The interference could be either purely physical or some electromagnetic influence. Whichever it is, it originates in either the conscious or the autonomic mind. I see no reason why the adverse instructions being received should not be countermanded.

# CHAPTER TWELVE
# THE IMPORTANCE OF
# SELF-HEALING

Our bodies effectively heal most of our ills most of the time. The body possesses mechanisms for safeguarding itself from dangerous intruders, for initiating growth to cover cuts and severe damage to tissue, bones, organs etc., and it sends out warning signs in the form of pain and fevers to induce the conscious mind to conform to the action required. But at times, when we are young, it fails, and increasingly so when we are old. There are many reasons for this, most of which we are well aware of; they concern our general behaviour, our eating habits, the pollution of our food and environment, and, of course, the defects we inherit from our parents and from the earth which we inhabit. So that, at times, the body needs help in its healing activities, and this it gets in very great measure and with marvels of ingenuity, scientific invention, and patient dedicated service, from all our medical practitioners. So much so that we are in danger of forgetting the part that the body itself must play in any form of healing. When it is forgetting to take the proper action, it must be reminded and given the necessary detail of the process that has to be initiated. This has to be done by the conscious mind and it is the way in which these directions can most effectively be given that this course of self-healing has described.

The system is, in no sense, a substitute for medical attention, except in the mildest of hurts where one has no business to take up the time of our overworked doctors; but it is a most valuable adjunct to whatever treatment may be advised. It is, in no sense, a panacea but it should become as natural a part of one's attention to bodily defects as, say, bandaging or applying a plaster to a cut. One often wishes one could do something to speed up and make more efficient a healing treatment. With this technique, that is just what one *can* do. If one cannot be certain of the potential of this technique, one must be clear about the limitations. The most obvious is that it does not deal with causes unless these are known, which they seldom are; it deals with symptoms. Also important is the necessity of knowing what process the body can bring into action to effect the healing. Certainly, the technique is most effective for all those minor ills that frequently need a doctor's attention; effective, that is, because the healing can be completed within a relatively short period. For more serious and deep-seated defects much patience and sometimes quite a long time is required, and the healing may have to be done in stages, dealing first with one aspect, and when that has been cleared up, tackling another. This is what I had to do when treating the arthritis in my hip.

It is possible either to avoid having to have other kinds of treatment or to work in conjunction with them. Modern orthodox medicine has reached a degree of excellence, both in its general practice and the various specialist techniques including much of the drug therapy that is in common use. Then there are the disciplines of massage, osteopathy, chiropractic, homoeopathy and other, at present, 'fringe' activities which are rapidly gaining ground. There is such a wide choice that a patient hardly thinks of turning to himself to bring about a cure. Much of the medical attention that is called for today would be unnecessary if the individual were able himself to get the natural healing processes of the body going, or to add to their effectiveness. And if orthodox or other treatment is being given, the patient can ensure that the body will be giving the maximum assistance.

There are many reasons why the body is not always able to deal with the situations that arise. Sometimes it is simply over-whelmed by the strength of the opposition. I recently experienced a case of this. For some time I had been aware of an inflammation of the prostate caused by some kind of infection, which I understand is common. As soon as I realized what was happening, I started a programme of scavenging to remove the infection. After a month to six weeks of this, the infection was still there, though much reduced. There were days when it had apparently died down altogether and then it would suddenly blow up again. I decided that the body needed help and asked my G.P. for some antibiotic treatment. The initial course was not successful, but a follow-up, coupled this time with a vigorous programme of scavenging, got rid of it altogether. The same thing, but on a larger and much more dangerous scale happens in the development of cancer. If the cancer is not detected by the body in its early stages (and this is one of the things about cancer which needs the most pressing research), it develops, or rather it can develop so quickly that the body's defensive mechanism is overwhelmed and cannot alone eliminate it.

This kind of thing can happen in many cases where the body is not quick enough to take the necessary action to overcome the threat, whether it be from a simple cut or a virulent disease germ. But I must emphasize once again that this self-healing technique should always be employed to assist whatever orthodox or other medical treatment is being carried out, since it brings the cells that have to take action wholeheartedly into the healing process. It is doing a little more than just saying to one-self: 'I am going to get well'. We have advanced very considerably in our standard of physical hygiene during the past two hundred years, this is a small advance in mental hygiene which I hope will be taken for granted before long, just as our drainage system is taken for granted now.

It is probable that many methods of treating disease and damage to the body that are now considered 'fringe' activities and unorthodox will, during the next few years, gradually be accepted by the medical fraternity as legitimate means of healing the body. This mind technique will fit in with all of them, it will simply be ensuring that the body does what it can to hasten the process of healing.

In addition to what is currently available, there will be important techniques in electro-, sound, and colour therapies, which are now only beginning to be used in special clinics. I do not mean the many uses of electro-therapy which are common to hospitals, clinics and specialists of all kinds, but the possibility of direct action on the electrical potential of organs to restore them to their original healthy levels. We shall then need a wise discrimination in order to decide which healing technique should be adopted in any particular case. But none of this will affect the mental technique described in this book, which can safely be carried out in conjunction with any of the others. After all, it is *your* body and you have control of it until something goes wrong with or overpowers the controlling mechanism. It is the conscious mind which has to re-establish that control, but reasonable medical assistance should always be welcome.

The technique I have outlined in the first few chapters is a good training for the efficient use of the mind, not only for self-healing, but for all the other mental activities of our daily life. We do not usually give the mind a chance to demonstrate its capabilities, mainly because we allow it to be deafened by extraneous noise and all kinds of interruptions, not least, those that stem from the uncontrolled chattering of our own thoughts. As one perseveres with a daily healing programme it will be found that the ability to focus will be enhanced, and one will 'feel' the power of the mind waiting to be delivered to the selected object. With continued daily practice, the rhythm of the programme will become firmly established and the conviction that one is getting the instructions across will grow.

It is not just faith, a sort of passive belief that is needed, but a positive use of the creative imagination. One has the tools (described in chapters 2 to 5) and one has the seed (the mental and visual instructions), so that it is the same kind of activity as cultivating one's garden, with the conviction that the plants that are now being sown will soon grow. The technique has to be taken out of the category of the extraordinary in one's mind to that of the common everyday expectation. We do not hesitate to believe, when we want to open a door, that the instructions we have to give to our muscles will be obeyed; it is that kind of conviction that we need to develop in giving the same kind of instructions to the cells and muscles of the body for the purpose of self-healing.

I want to stress once again the importance of getting a diagnosis from a doctor or a specialist in certain cases. For this technique to be successful, it is absolutely essential that one is directing the body to do the right thing in the right place. If it is a question of removing a polyp, a cyst, an area of calcified tissue etc., it increases the effectiveness of a programme if the location of the tissue to be removed is known with some accuracy. This will enable the mind-picture to focus on the spot where action has to be taken. When receiving a read-out' on an X-ray from an orthopaedic surgeon, for instance, I asked that the positions of the calcified tissue shown up by the X-ray should be related to the actual position in the body, by pressing a finger on the spot. The vaguer your idea of the position in the body where action is to be taken, the less effective that action will be. This accuracy is not always possible because doctors very often do not know exactly what is going on.

As an instance, I would mention the complete loss of taste and smell from which I suffer. Ear, Nose and Throat specialists do not know the cause of this, neither do they know where the breakdown in the rather complex olfactory system has occurred. Consequently, there is very little one can do about it. I have tried various programmes aimed at different parts of the system, but without any effect. They were obviously not doing what was needed to bring about the recovery of the sense. In order to be successful with this technique, it is essential to have a diagnosis of what has happened to produce the harmful effect, and what the body could or should be doing to put matters right. With that kind of information, you can get going with a suitable programme.

I hope that, with the information given in this book, there will be many people trying out programmes to overcome defects and ills of all kinds. The experience they will gain will be of great value to all, and it is essential that this information is collected and analyzed, in order to find out what improvements in the technique have been discovered, which new programmes have been successful and which have failed. The smallest details of modifications to the 'think-speak' and 'think-see' given in the various programmes are important; for instance, effective ways of visualizing the action of the phagocytic cells would be helpful. The kind of instruction that can be given to indicate that a growth, whether it be a polyp, a cyst, calcified or fibrous tissue, is harmful, foreign, and a proper target for the scavenging cells would, I think, increase very greatly the effectiveness of such programmes.

There is so much that others will find out that will be valuable for the development of this technique, that I ask all who think they may have something to contribute to write to me at the address given at the end of this chapter. I shall be happy to co-ordinate all the information that comes in. This will enable me to do two things; first, to give better advice to all those who write with a problem, and secondly, to see that all the up-to-date information is given the publicity it merits.

Rear Admiral E. H. Shattock,<br>
The Mill House,<br>
Newark,<br>
Ripley,<br>
Surrey GU23 6DP.

# INDEX